Who Pooped in Central Park?™

WRITTEN BY
GARY D. ROBSON

ILLUSTRATED BY
ROBERT RATH

FARCOUNTRY
PRESS

To my father:
I wish you had made it to your
100th birthday this year to see me finally
writing a book set in New York. – Gary

Thanks to Lucy, Thomas, and Claire
for being great models and poop experts! – Robert

CENTRAL PARK

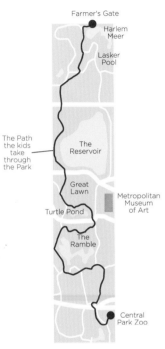

Farmer's Gate

Harlem
Meer

Lasker
Pool

The Path
the kids
take
through
the Park

The Reservoir

Great
Lawn

Turtle Pond

Metropolitan
Museum
of Art

The
Ramble

Central
Park Zoo

ISBN 13: 978-1-56037-654-5
© 2016 by Farcountry Press
Text © 2016 by Gary D. Robson

For more information on our books, write:
Farcountry Press, P.O. Box 5630, Helena, MT 59604;
call (800) 821-3874; or visit www.farcountrypress.com.

Manufactured by:
Bang Printing
3323 Oak Street
Brainerd, MN 56401
In April 2016

 Produced and printed in the United States of America.

PIGEON

"Are you kids going to be okay by yourselves for a while?"

"Yes, Mr. Montano," said Emma, Jackson, and Lily. Mr. Montano looked at Tony.

"Do you have your phone, Tony?" Dad asked.

"Yes, Dad," Tony sighed. "It's in my backpack. We've been here a hundred times. We'll be fine!"

WHITE-FOOTED MOUSE

"What should we see first?" Jackson asked, "The red pandas?"

"I *love* the red pandas," Lily said. "They are so *cute!*"

AMERICAN ROBIN

Emma pulled on Tony's arm. "You're right, Tony. We've been to the zoo, like, a *million* times. Let's explore something new!"

"Let's go to the Pond!" Tony said. "We might catch a crayfish!"

"I am not sticking my hand in that gross water," Lily answered.

"Hey, the water doesn't look icky at all!" said Emma.

"You're not allowed to catch crayfish in the Park anyway," said Jackson.

RED-BELLIED WOODPECKER

THE STRAIGHT POOP

If you see a crayfish, don't pick it up! Crayfish don't like being handled, and a pinch from those claws would hurt.

MONARCH
BUTTERFLY

"Stay clear of that bush," said a man working on the trail. "I think there are rats back there."

Emma said, "How do you know?" and at the same time Lily said, "Who are you?"

NORWAY
RAT

THE STRAIGHT POOP

Rats love garbage! Help keep Central Park clean. Always put your trash in a trash can. Never approach a rat, even if it acts friendly. Like any other wild animal, it may bite and could carry diseases.

RED-WINGED
BLACKBIRD

"I'm Lawton," the man said, "and I can tell what animals are around by their scat and tracks."

"*Scat* is what scientists call animal poop," Jackson said. "I read that at the library."

"That's right," said Lawton. "See here. Those footprints and poop are from a rat."

"Look! There's a rat right there," Tony yelled.

"No, it's a beaver!" Emma added.

"Actually, that's a muskrat," Lawton told them. "The name may have 'rat' in it, but they aren't really rats."

"You're lucky to see the muskrat—they're pretty scarce and they mostly stay in the water," Lawton explained.

"Some Native American legends say that it was a muskrat that swam to the bottom of the sea and brought up the mud to create the Earth."

BLACK SWALLOWTAIL BUTTERFLY

MUSKRAT

NORWAY RAT

The kids wandered away from Lawton toward the Mall.
Suddenly Tony shoved Lily sideways.

"Watch where you're going!" Lily shouted.

"Sorry," Tony said. "But you were about to step in that poop!"

"Scat," Jackson reminded him. "This looks like it's from a big dog . . . or maybe a coyote!"

"People are supposed to pick up after their dogs," Lily said. "Leaving dog poop there is *disgusting*."

BORDER COLLIE

THE STRAIGHT POOP

Every few years, someone sees a coyote in Central Park. Coyotes are common in upstate New York, and a few even live in New York City. Coyote scat looks like dog poop but has fur and bits of bones in it from the small animals they eat.

"Hey guys," Emma said, "There's more rat poop over here."

"I don't think a rat made that," said Lily. "I bet it's squirrel poop."

"That makes sense," said Tony. "Rats and squirrels are both rodents, so their—"

"*Scat*," said Jackson.

"Yeah, their scat looks almost the same," finished Tony.

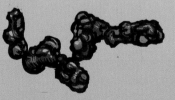

SQUIRREL SCAT   RACCOON SCAT

JELLYBEANS

EASTERN GRAY SQUIRREL

"I wonder why the squirrel is hiding under the tree?" said Lily.

Tony looked up from the squirrel. "I'll bet that's why it's hiding," he said pointing at a big bird in the sky. "Hawks eat squirrels, right?"

"I wonder if that's the famous hawk that has a nest on the building over there?" Emma asked.

"Pale Male?" asked Jackson. "Our school library has a book about him."

THE STRAIGHT POOP

A red-tailed hawk named "Pale Male" settled on the edge of Central Park in the 1990s and raised dozens of babies (called "eyasses") there. His descendants live all over New York City.

"This poop is gigantic!" Lily said. "What animal in the Park is that big?"

Jackson said, "Horses! That scat is from the horses pulling those carriages."

A friendly voice behind them said, "A cleaning crew will sweep that up later."

HORSE TRACKS

"How come you're riding a horse?" Tony asked the police officer.

"Horses can go a lot of places that cars and motorcycles can't," she answered. "And up here I can keep an eye on things."

"Besides," she laughed, "I love riding old Gwen. She and I are best friends."

THE STRAIGHT
POOP

Six mounted police units are scattered throughout the city, including a team of officers that patrols Central Park.

"Hey!" said Jackson. "Is that guy fishing?"

"Cool!" said Emma. "Let's check it out."

CANADA GEESE

"Ew, this is gross," Lily said. "Is this animal poop, too?"

"Looks like it came out of a goose," said Tony. "There's one pooping over there."

"Yuk!" said Lily.

THE STRAIGHT POOP

An adult Canada goose can produce up to two pounds of poop per day!

MALLARD (FEMALE)

MALLARD (MALE)

BLACK-CROWNED NIGHT HERON

KILLDEER

"Are you letting that fish go?" Tony asked. "How come?"

"Because those are the rules," the man replied. "When you catch a fish in Central Park, you have to let it go."

"What kind of fish is that, sir?" Tony continued.

THE STRAIGHT POOP

Some people dump their pet fish in Park waters, even though they are not supposed to. Some goldfish in the Lake are really big!

BLUEGILL

AMERICAN BULLFROG

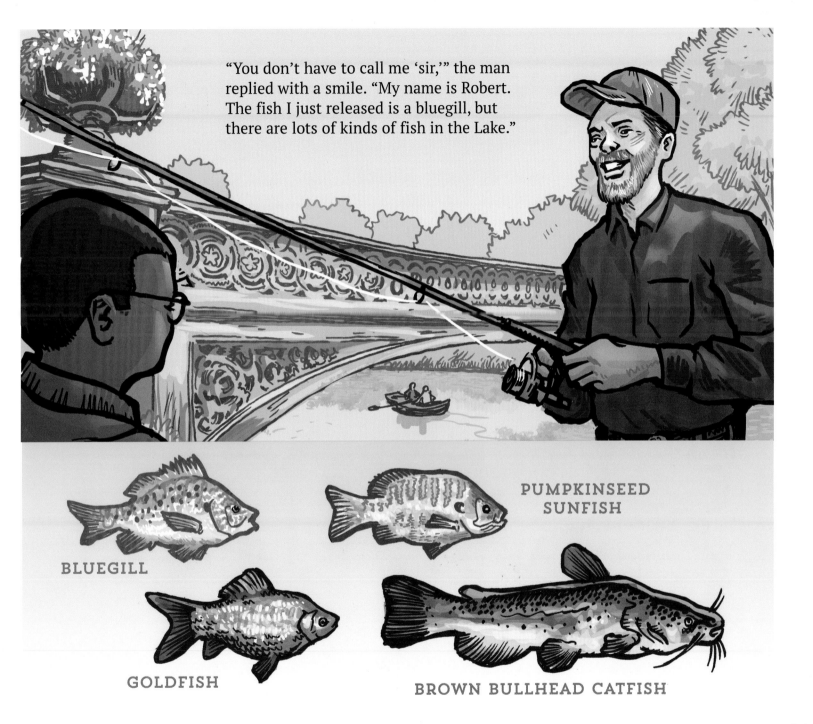

"You don't have to call me 'sir,'" the man replied with a smile. "My name is Robert. The fish I just released is a bluegill, but there are lots of kinds of fish in the Lake."

BLUEGILL

PUMPKINSEED SUNFISH

GOLDFISH

BROWN BULLHEAD CATFISH

"Ha, ha, ha, ha!"
came a girlish laugh.

Tony spun around. "Are you laughing at me?"

"It's not us," said Emma.

LAUGHING GULL

NORTHERN CARDINAL

"It's that bird on the bridge," said Robert. "They're called laughing gulls because they sound like someone laughing."

"Ha, ha, ha, ha!" said the gull. The kids all laughed along.

RACCOONS

THE STRAIGHT POOP

Raccoons like to poop in the same place as other raccoons, kind of like public bathrooms . . . but for raccoons. If you find a "raccoon latrine," don't go near the poop—it contains tiny round-worm eggs that can make you really sick.

"Why are there so many pigeons here?" Lily asked.

"I think that big building is the Met," Jackson said. "We went there on a field trip and there were tons of pigeons."

THE STRAIGHT POOP

The Metropolitan Museum of Art ("The Met") is the biggest art museum in the United States. Pigeons flock here to look for food (and to poop on people).

"I've been to this place before!" Tony said.
"It's called Turtle Pond."

"How come?" Emma asked.

AUTUMN MEADOWHAWK DRAGONFLY

BLUE DASHER DRAGONFLY

GREEN DARNER DRAGONFLY

BULLFROG

25

EASTERN KINGBIRD

RED-EARED SLIDER

THE STRAIGHT POOP

Like the goldfish, a lot of the red-eared sliders here are people's pets that were dumped in the Park. Most abandoned pets don't live very long.

27

"Hey, look!" said Tony. "There's one of those animals that looks at its shadow to tell if winter is over."

"A groundhog," said Emma.

GROUNDHOG

THE STRAIGHT POOP

Groundhogs (also called woodchucks) build long, underground tunnels with special rooms just for pooping, so you won't find much groundhog poop above the ground.

"What's that lady doing with the binoculars?" Lily asked. "Let's go see!"

RED-BELLIED WOODPECKER

THE STRAIGHT POOP

If you poke apart woodpecker scat with a pencil, you'll find lots of bug parts, since that's what woodpeckers eat. But don't touch animal poop with your fingers!

29

"What are you looking at?" Lily asked her. "Are you a painter? Is this your painting?"

The woman laughed. "My name is Dominique and yes, I'm a painter."

"I'm painting this scarlet tanager, but I can't get close without scaring him. That's why I use binoculars," she explained.

SCARLET TANAGER

THE STRAIGHT POOP

Most birds won't sit still for a portrait, so painters often photograph a bird to better see details like eye color and the shape of its beak.

31

"There are a lot of beautiful songbirds here if you look carefully," she told the kids.

"Can we look?" Tony asked. "We'll be careful!"

STARLING

HERMIT THRUSH

EUROPEAN STARLING

SCARLET TANAGER

NORTHERN CARDINAL

BLUE JAY

One by one, Dominique helped the children find birds through the binoculars.

EASTERN GRAY SQUIRREL

EASTERN CHIPMUNK

"You can see more than birds here," Dominique told them. "Look—there's a chipmunk!"

34

CHIPMUNK
TRACKS

FIELD
CRICKET

CHIPMUNK
SCAT

THE STRAIGHT POOP

Chipmunks live in burrows in the ground. They eat seeds, nuts, insects, worms, and bird eggs, carrying the food in their cheeks back to their burrow.

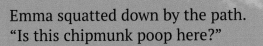

Emma squatted down by the path. "Is this chipmunk poop here?"

Dominique looked over Emma's shoulder. "Yes, and you can even see their footprints in that muddy spot."

"For many years, no one saw any chipmunks in Central Park," Dominique said, "but now they're back."

"It's getting cold," Lily said. "Do you have a jacket in your pack, Tony?"

"You can use my hoodie," he said. Then, as he pulled out the sweatshirt, Tony cried, "Oh, no!"

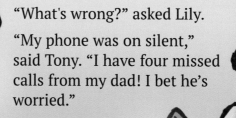

"What's wrong?" asked Lily.

"My phone was on silent," said Tony. "I have four missed calls from my dad! I bet he's worried."

EASTERN
SCREECH
OWL

NESSUS
SPHINX
MOTH

Tony called his father. "Hi Dad! Yeah, we're ready to go. But I'm not sure exactly where we are."

A woman nearby overheard. "This path will take you around Harlem Meer to the Farmers Gate," she said. "You can meet your dad there."

ILIA UNDERWING

NESSUS SPHINX MOTH

"Thanks, lady!" Tony said after he hung up. "What are you looking at on that tree?"

"My name is Ruth," she said, "and I'm looking at moths."

"Not at that owl over your head?" Emma asked?

THE STRAIGHT POOP

There are some big, amazing moths in Central Park that you won't see unless you look carefully after dark,

LUNA MOTH

BLACK WITCH MOTH

EASTERN SCREECH OWL

"I was so interested in the moths, I didn't even look up!" Ruth said. "He's a beautiful little screech owl. I was just getting ready to look for bats. Would you like to join me?"

"Bats?" said Jackson. "Cool!"

THE STRAIGHT POOP

Eastern screech owls were reintro-duced (brought back) in Central Park in 1998. "Owl pellets" that you might find under a tree aren't scat—they're bones, fur, and feathers that owls cough up after eating small animals whole.

EASTERN FIREFLIES

"You can tell it's time for the bats when you see the fireflies and hear the crickets and cicadas," Ruth told them.

DOG-DAY CICADA

FIELD CRICKETS

Tony called out, "There's a bat!"

Bat poop is called "guano." People spread it on their gardens to help the plants grow.

EASTERN RED BAT

SWEETHEART UNDERWING MOTH

41

BIG
BROWN
BAT

"There are lots of bats in Central Park, but they usually don't come out until after dark," Ruth said. "Some bats are big, some are small, and some have colorful fur."

EASTERN
RED BAT

LITTLE
BROWN
BAT

BIG
BROWN
BAT

"I had no idea there were so
many different kinds of bats!"
Jackson said.

TRI-COLORED
BAT

THE STRAIGHT POOP

Each hair on a tri-colored bat is black
at the base, yellow in the middle,
and brown at the tip. These tiny bats
weigh about as much as a nickel.

43

"Hi, kids," said Mr. Montano.
"You had quite a long day.
I hope you had fun."

"It was kind of a poopy day in the Park," Tony said, winking at his friends.

"But in a good way!" Emma added.

MUSKRAT

BACK
FRONT

The rear paw with five toes is much larger than front with four toes. Look for a line in the track from the dragging tail.

Muskrats make mounds of dirt to poop on, often near a rock or tree stump they mark with their scent.

NORWAY RAT

BACK
FRONT

Track shows five toes on the rear paw and four on the front. The outer toes often point straight out to the sides.

Rat pellets collect around the rats' nests and along trails they follow.

EASTERN GRAY SQUIRREL

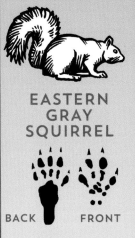

BACK
FRONT

Tracks show four toes on front paws and five on the rear, usually in a hopping pattern.

Look for small, oval scat on tree stumps or logs where squirrels feed.

EASTERN CHIPMUNK

FRONT

BACK

Tracks show four toes on the front paws and five toes on the rear with the three middle toes lined up close together.

Scat may be linked or individual pellets about the size of rice grains.

GROUNDHOG

FRONT

BACK

Tracks show four toes on the front paws and five on the rear, with deep toenail marks.

You probably won't see groundhog scat because they poop underground or bury it.

& NOTES

HORSE

You might find C-shaped horse tracks in the dirt alongside park roads and paths.

Scat can be runny or dry "apples" with bits of hay. Color ranges from green to brown.

RED-TAILED HAWK

In winter, you might get lucky and see wing and tail marks in the snow where a hawk has landed on prey.

Scat is white and runny, often in streaks below a nest or perch. Hawks also cough up pellets of hair and small bones.

RACCOON

Tracks show five toes on front and rear paws, often with toenails.

FRONT
BACK

Scat is tubular with blunt ends, similar to a small dog's. Often contains bits of whatever they've eaten: seeds, nuts, popcorn, pepperoni pizza....

CANADA GOOSE

Tracks show three long toes, sometimes with webbing marks in between.

Scat is green, brown, or black and tends to whiten as it dries.

DOMESTIC DOG

FRONT
BACK

Tracks show a heel pad and four toes with toenails. May be little or large depending on the size of dog.

Scat is brown and tubular with blunt or tapered ends, often breaking into segments.

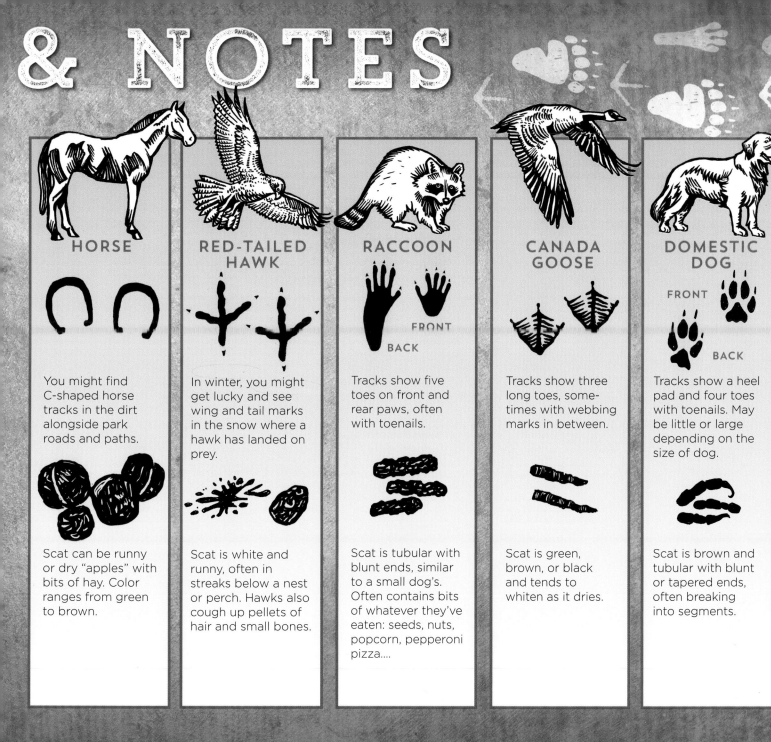

ABOUT THE AUTHOR & ILLUSTRATOR

GARY D. ROBSON

GARY D. ROBSON was born in the great state of New York, and now lives in Montana, not too far from Yellowstone Park. He has written dozens of books and hundreds of articles, mostly related to science and technology.

www.GaryDRobson.com

ROBERT RATH

ROBERT RATH is a book designer and illustrator living in Bozeman, Montana. Although he has worked with Scholastic Books, Lucasfilm and The History Channel, his favorite project is keeping up with his family.

Who Pooped?

BOOKS IN THE WHO POOPED? SERIES:

Olympic
Cascades
Glacier
Black Hills
Northwoods
Acadia
Redwoods
Grand Teton
Yellowstone
Central Park
Yosemite
Rocky Mountain
Shenandoah
Sequoia/Kings Canyon
Red Rock Canyon
Death Valley
Grand Canyon
Colorado Plateau
Great Smoky Mountains
Sonoran Desert
Big Bend